The Rechargeables

Eat Move Sleep

MISSIONDAY

To my wife, Ashley, who dedicates her life and career to creating a positive charge for kids.

Tom Rath
Author

I want to specially dedicate this book to my mother, Cristina, who devoted her life to her profession as a nutritionist and taught me the value of staying healthy.

Carlos Aón
Illustrator

ISBN: 9781939714046

Library of Congress Control Number: 2014921529

Copyright © Tom Rath

Illustrated by Carlos Aón
Color Assistant, Laura Lazzati

Design and production by Cheryl Blum

First Printing: 2015
10 9 8 7 6 5 4 3 2 1

Bulk purchase discounts, special editions, and customized excerpts are available direct from the publisher. For information about books for educational, business, or promotional purposes, please email: inquiries@missionday.com

To book Tom Rath for a speaking engagement, contact Missionday Speakers Bureau: speaking@missionday.com

Author's website: www.tomrath.org

Printed in China

The Rechargeables
Eat Move Sleep

by
Tom Rath

illustrated by
Carlos Aón

4

In the village of Verve, a mysterious thing has occurred . . . all of the people are completely still.

On the outskirts of town, a young girl named Poppy is sitting on a hilltop when a strong gust of wind blows her over.

6

Poppy's stiff body hits the ground and starts to roll.

As she rolls, her eyes begin to open.
Poppy can feel her arms hitting
the ground with each turn.

Poppy struggles to stand up. As she pushes with her arms, she feels a positive charge. Poppy looks up and sees someone leaning against a tree.

Who is this boy? she wonders.

She takes a step toward him, then another. And with each
step, she gains strength. Poppy shakes the boy. Nothing.
She pushes him over thinking it might help. It does not.

Then Poppy notices a house. She walks over to see
if anyone is inside.

As Poppy walks into the dusty house, she sees a man sitting at a table and a woman on the couch.

She doesn't know who the people are or why they're not moving.

Poppy shakes the woman. Nothing.

10

When she goes to shake the man, she notices something written on his notepad:

What you DO gives you energy.

Poppy thinks about the message for a minute, then gets an idea.

11

"Wh . . . wh . . . what happened? Where am I? Who are you?" the boy mumbles.

That is about the only question Poppy knows the answer to. "My name is Poppy. What's yours?"

"Uh . . . Simon, I think?"

Poppy sees a red light on Simon's shirt that was not there before. As he gets up and takes a few steps, the light turns a dim yellow.

Poppy then looks down at her own shirt and notices that she has a glowing yellow light as well!

Poppy and Simon wander down the road toward the village, hoping to find others who are charged. With each step they take, Poppy and Simon seem to have more energy.

"I think your light is turning green as we walk faster," Simon notices.

"You're right, it is!" she exclaims. "Think you can run?"

"I don't know, but I'll try," says Simon.

After running down the road for a few minutes, Simon's light turns green as well. So they keep running, faster and faster.

They think running might give them an endless supply of energy.

But it does not.

Confused and growing tired, Poppy says, "Just moving won't keep us charged long enough. We should write that down, in case we lose our charge."

"Good idea! We need paper and a pencil," says Simon.

"I saw some at the house by the hill. Let's head back before we lose more energy," replies Poppy.

It takes a long time, but they make it back.

Simon grabs the notepad with the message,
turns the page over, and writes:

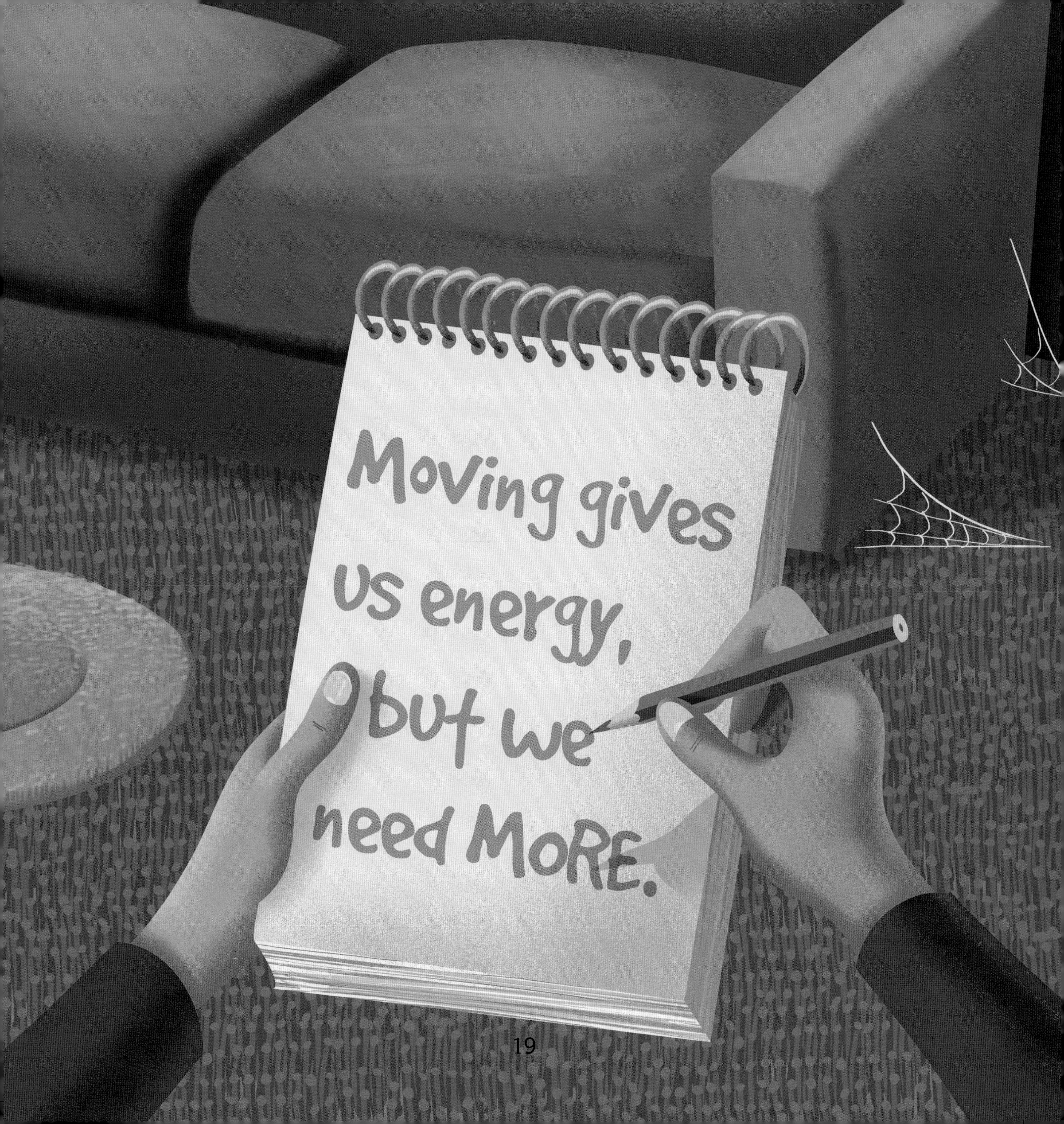
Moving gives
us energy,
but we
need MORE.

There has to be another answer to the mystery of why they lost their charge. As Simon thinks about the problem, he notices his stomach is rumbling.

"Maybe we're just hungry? Let's see if we can find some food in here."

Poppy and Simon go through all the cabinets and drawers in the kitchen. They put everything they can find on the counter.

All of the fresh food in the refrigerator has gone bad, but there are two bottles of soda left and plenty of bags and boxes of food.

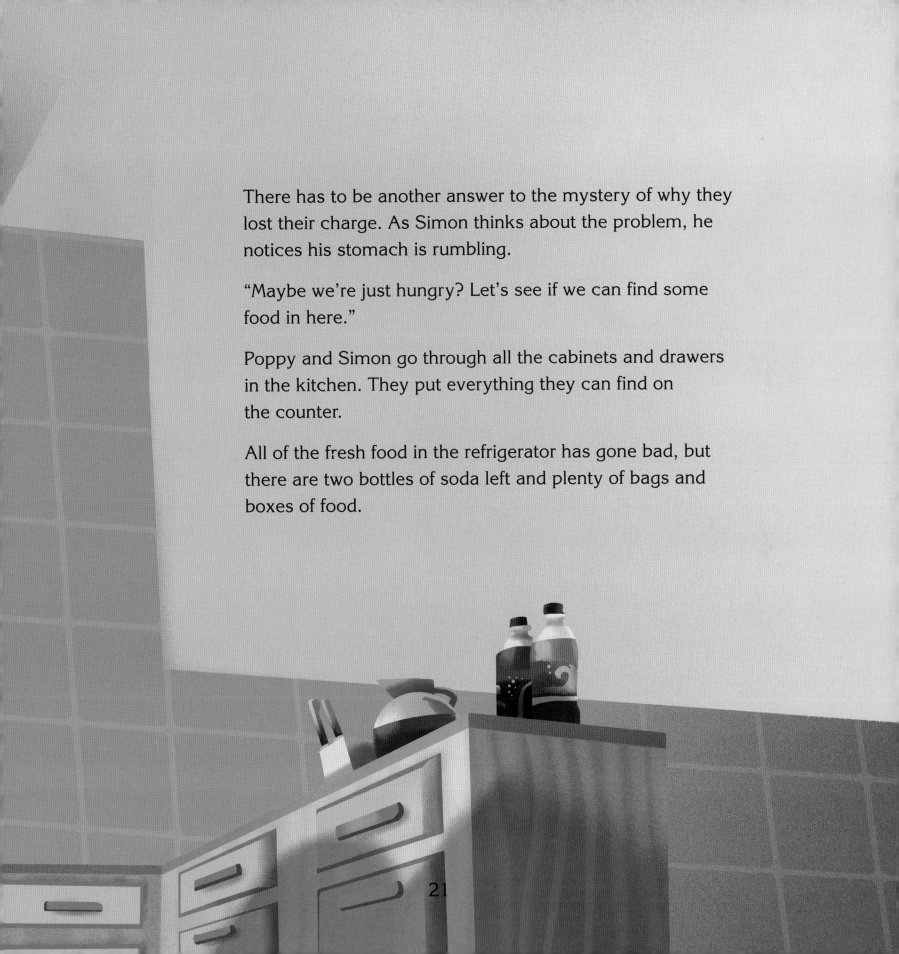

Simon starts eating some cookies. Poppy takes a big gulp of soda and opens a bag of potato chips.

These foods give them more energy at first, so they keep eating.

But after a while, they both get a stomachache and begin to lose their charge.

"Do you think we are eating the right food?" asks Poppy.

"It tastes good to me," answers Simon with his mouth full of cookies.

Then he loses the rest of his charge . . . and goes completely still.

Poppy drags Simon out the door and rolls him down the hill, thinking that will give him a small charge.

But this time, it does not.

So Poppy tries rolling him down another hill.

24

Simon rolls right into a garden filled with fruits and vegetables.

When Poppy runs down the hill, she notices that Simon has a small charge. But he will need more to get moving again.

As Simon struggles to get up, Poppy has another idea.

"Look at all these fresh fruits and vegetables. Maybe they will help."

After just a few bites of an apple, Simon has enough energy to explore the rest of the garden with Poppy.

With each bite of *these* foods, Poppy and Simon gain energy.

"If we take some of these foods with us, they may give us enough of a charge to make it to the village," says Simon.

"Let's go right now!" Poppy exclaims.

27

Off they go, snacking on apples, berries, and carrots along the
way. This time they make it!

They hope to find someone else moving around, but the entire village is still. None of the people have a charge.

"It's getting dark. We should go back to the house," says Poppy.

As they walk along, Poppy and Simon yawn at the same time.

They are getting sleepy.

When they get to the house, Poppy says, "We better get some rest. But write down what we learned, in case we lose our charge again."

Simon grabs the notepad and writes:

Then they both fall fast asleep.

When Poppy and Simon wake up the next morning, they feel even better than they did the day before.

Simon looks at Poppy and asks her, "Do you think sleeping gave us more energy?"

"I think so, because I feel great!" replies Poppy.

"I can even remember things now," states Poppy.
"You are my brother!"

"Yep, and those must be our parents. It's all starting to make sense," says Simon. "So how do we get Mom and Dad recharged?"

"I think I know how!" exclaims Poppy.

"Ready?" asks Poppy.

"Let 'em roll!"

34

"Wh . . . wh . . . where . . . am . . . I? Who are you?" Mom asks as Poppy and Simon lean over her.

"Wha . . . what is going on?" Dad mumbles.

Poppy and Simon can hardly wait to tell their parents all they learned. But they know their mom and dad need to build up their energy levels first.

"Let's take them to the garden," says Simon.

"Once you start moving around, you will get a positive charge and feel better," Poppy explains to her parents.

38

By the time they get to the garden, Mom and Dad feel better, but they still don't remember much.

"If you eat these fruits and vegetables, it will help," says Simon.

They fill up with fresh food and walk up the hill to the house. The entire family is feeling like new again.

When they go inside, Simon can't wait to ask his dad about the note he was writing.

"What were you trying to tell us, Dad?" asks Simon as he hands him the notepad.

"We learned that moving around during the day and sleeping well at night gave us energy," says Dad. "But I guess that wasn't enough."

As Poppy looks at the counter filled with packaged foods that did not help her and Simon recharge, she adds, "I think it's also about eating the *right* foods."

"That has to be it!" says Mom. Dad nods his head in agreement.

That night before bed, Simon grabs the notepad and writes:

Eat right,
move more,
and sleep
well
for energy.

The next morning, the entire family wakes up fully charged.

As Dad gets breakfast ready, he asks, "What should we do today?"

"I have an idea," says Poppy. "Now that we know how to stay charged, let's energize the whole village!"

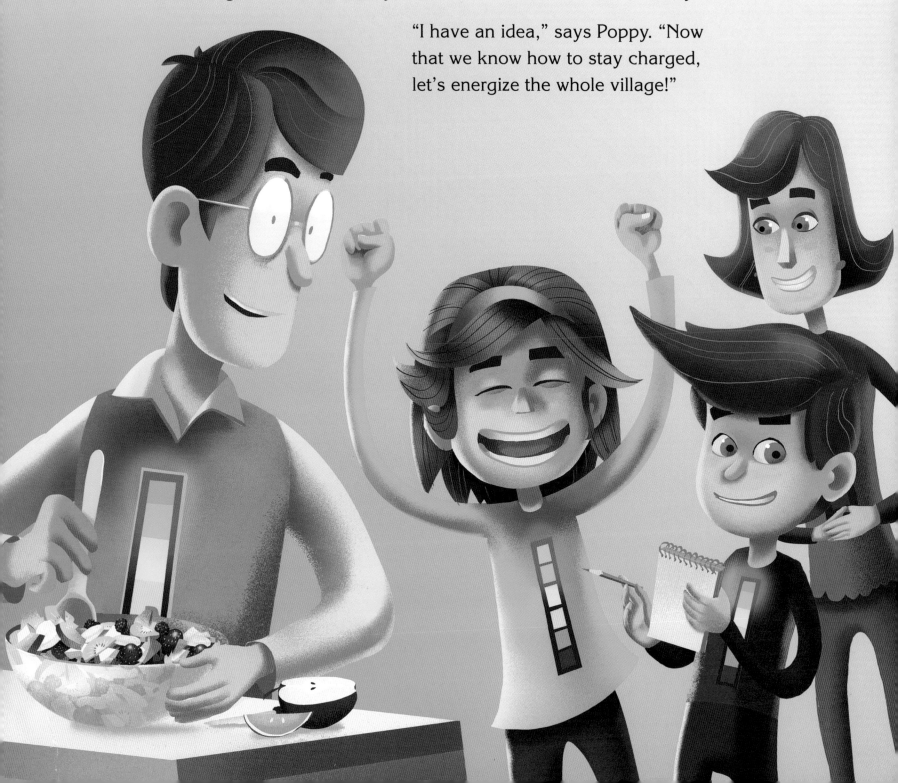

Now, a question for you:

What gets YOU fully charged?

Talk about these questions and remember to ALWAYS BE CHARGING!

EAT:

What foods give you more energy throughout the day?

MOVE:

Which activities give you a positive charge?

SLEEP:

What helps you get a good night's sleep ?

EAT:

What is your
favorite
vegetable?

MOVE:

What sport
or game
do you like
to play?

SLEEP:

What time
do you go to
sleep?

Talk about these questions and remember to ALWAYS BE CHARGING!

Ideas for Discussion

Eating healthy, moving around, and sleeping well at night keeps us fully charged.

Questions: Why is it important to focus on all three areas (eat, move, sleep) together? What happens if you don't do one? How does it affect the other two?

Action: Change one thing you do regularly to eat, move, or sleep better today. Share with a friend.

EATING: Healthy fruits, vegetables, nuts, and whole foods give us lasting energy to be our best.

Questions: Have you ever gotten a stomachache from eating certain foods? Do you think your body was trying to tell you something?

Action: Make a list of foods that give you energy *and* are good for you. Make a list of bad foods that drain your energy. Then, independently, write down what you normally eat for breakfast, lunch, and dinner. Select a good food to eat more of and a bad food to avoid. Share your selections with your class or your friends.

MOVING: Physical activity gives our bodies and brains a charge.

Questions: Do you feel better after going outside for recess and getting activity? What can you do to get a little more activity every day?

Action: In small groups or with a partner, think of activities that will give you energy right now (e.g., marching in place, jumping jacks, the hokey pokey dance, etc.). Share and demonstrate these activities.

SLEEPING: A good night's sleep helps us reset our bodies and get ready for the new and exciting day ahead of us.

Questions: If you go to bed late, how do you feel the next morning? What can you do to make sure you have a good night's sleep and feel fully rested?

Action: Share your bedtime routine with a friend. Talk about what time you go to bed, what you do to get ready for bed, and what you do before turning off the lights.

Optional Discussion Questions:

Poppy and Simon are the problem solvers in *The Rechargeables*.

Questions: Can you think of a time when you helped to solve a problem? How did it make you feel? If you were in Poppy and Simon's place, would you do anything differently than they did? What if the big gust of wind had not blown Poppy down the hill? Would the village of Verve stay uncharged forever?

Action: With a partner, think of another way the town could become charged again. Share with the class.

Stickers and More!

In the back of this book, you will find stickers that can be used as recognition for days when kids are fully charged, when they create a positive charge, or just for fun!

Visit **www.tomrath.org/therechargeables** to:

- Read central points from the book *Eat Move Sleep: How Small Choices Lead to Big Changes* about healthy foods, ways to add activity, and tips on how to sleep better

- Download discussion cards to use with kids and in classrooms

- Find extended classroom activities based on *The Rechargeables*

- Complete the free Eat Move Sleep Plan based on the nonfiction book

- Review hundreds of resources, references, and links on healthy eating, moving, and sleeping

- Find programs for creating themed and semester-long activities based around this book

I am
fully
charged!

I am
fully
charged!

I am
fully
charged!

I am
fully
charged!